Learn to DRAW

Drawing
Dragons

Jorge Santillan and Sarah Eason

Gareth Stevens
Publishing

Please visit our website, www.garethstevens.com. For a free color catalog of all our high-quality books, call toll free 1-800-542-2595 or fax 1-877-542-2596.

Library of Congress Cataloging-in-Publication Data

Eason, Sarah.
 Drawing dragons / Sarah Eason.
    pages cm. — (Learn to draw)
ISBN 978-1-4339-9533-0 (pbk.)
ISBN 978-1-4339-9534-7 (6-pack)
ISBN 978-1-4339-9532-3 (library binding)
1. Dragons in art–Juvenile literature. 2. Drawing—Technique—Juvenile literature. I. Title.
 NC825.D72E27 2013
 743'.87—dc23
                                2012048246

Published in 2014 by
Gareth Stevens Publishing
111 East 14th Street, Suite 349
New York, NY 10003

© 2014 Gareth Stevens Publishing

Produced for Gareth Stevens by Calcium Creative Ltd
Illustrated by Jorge Santillan
Designed by Paul Myerscough
Edited by Rachel Blount

Printed in the United States of America

CPSIA compliance information: Batch CS13GS: For further information contact Gareth Stevens, New York, New York at 1-800-542-2595.

Contents

Learn to Draw!

People around the world have believed in dragons for thousands of years. These fierce, all-powerful creatures have huge bodies, curling, razor-sharp claws, sweeping tails, and jaws lined with daggerlike teeth! Some dragons breathe fire, other dragons live in oceans and lakes. Many have wings so they can fly high in the air and sweep through the skies. Discover more about these amazing creatures—then learn how to draw them, too.

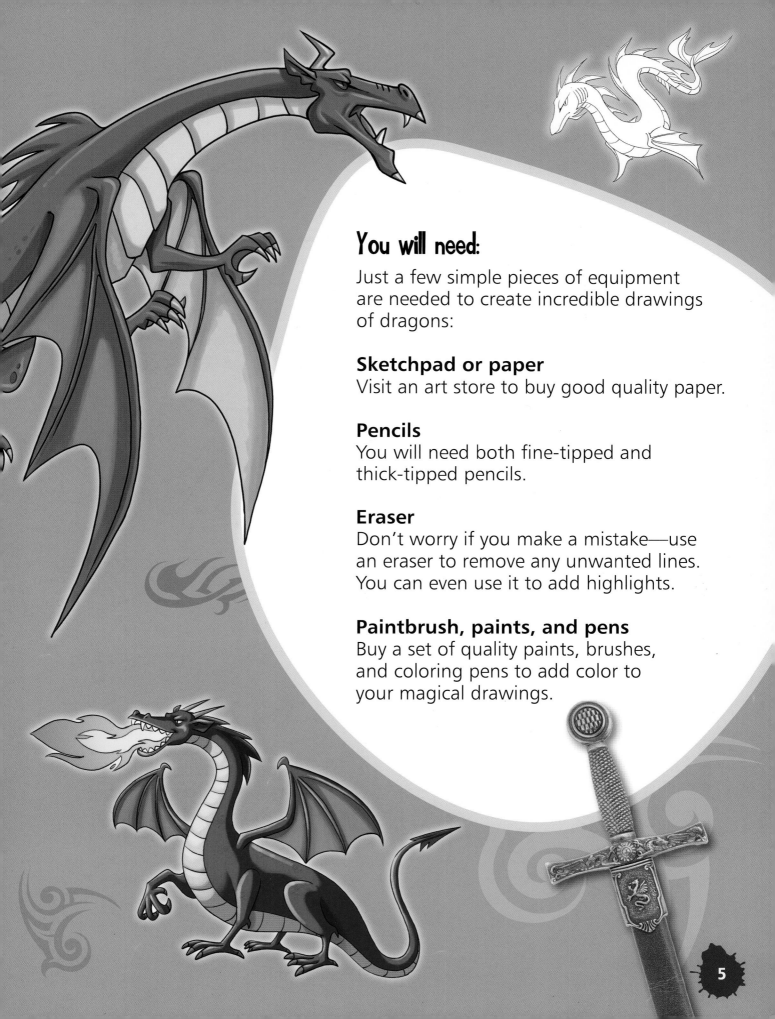

You will need:

Just a few simple pieces of equipment are needed to create incredible drawings of dragons:

Sketchpad or paper
Visit an art store to buy good quality paper.

Pencils
You will need both fine-tipped and thick-tipped pencils.

Eraser
Don't worry if you make a mistake—use an eraser to remove any unwanted lines. You can even use it to add highlights.

Paintbrush, paints, and pens
Buy a set of quality paints, brushes, and coloring pens to add color to your magical drawings.

Magical Dragons

In many ancient stories, dragons are said to have magical powers. Dragons may use their magic to disguise themselves as human beings, so they can walk unnoticed among people. Powerful dragons can even talk!

Step 1

Draw your magical dragon in an upright pose, with its forelegs held out before it. Draw the body, hind legs, and feet. Then draw the neck, head, wings, and the dragon's long, curving tail.

Step 2

Now give your dragon a more rounded outline and erase the lines from step 1. Draw the features of its face, the horns on its head, its ears, claws, curved wings and the daggerlike tip of its tail.

Step 3

Now draw the outline of the eyes, nostrils, the mouth, and the ridge of scales on the dragon's back and tail. Then add the lines on the enormous wings.

Step 4

Draw the teeth and the markings on the snout, chest, and belly. Add detail to the claws.

Step 5

Now shade your magical dragon's body, head, legs, wings, and its sweeping tail.

Step 6

Color the horns, belly, and chest yellow. Use a deep gold color for the inside of the wings, and pink for the rest of the dragon. Give it yellow eyes and gray claws.

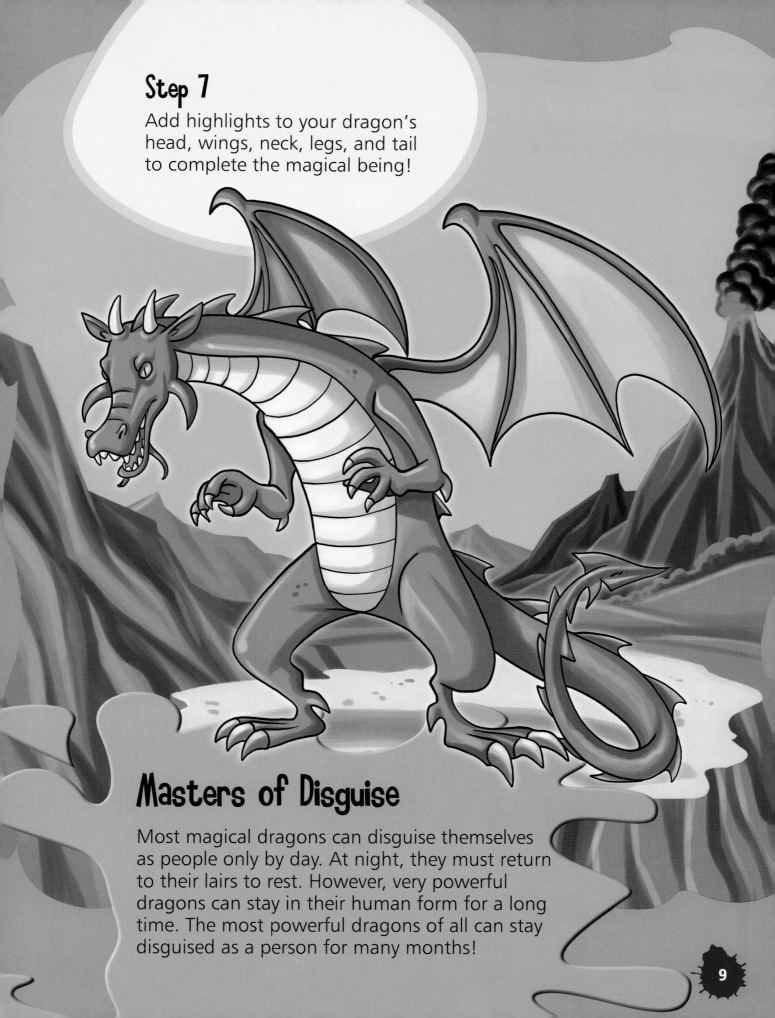

Step 7

Add highlights to your dragon's head, wings, neck, legs, and tail to complete the magical being!

Masters of Disguise

Most magical dragons can disguise themselves as people only by day. At night, they must return to their lairs to rest. However, very powerful dragons can stay in their human form for a long time. The most powerful dragons of all can stay disguised as a person for many months!

Wicked Dragons

Just like wizards, some dragons are good and others are wicked! These dragons use their magical powers to harm people. There are many stories about dragons that sweep across the land, breathing fire that burns villages and scorches the earth.

Step 1

Draw this evil dragon in a standing pose. Draw the body, legs, feet, neck, head, and tail. Draw triangles for the wings and a triangle for the tip of the tail.

Step 2

Now go over the rough drawings from step 1 to give your dragon a more finished outline. Mark the features of the face and ears, and draw the shape of the jaws. Add scales on the neck.

Step 3

Now watch your dragon start to come to life as you add the ragged crest behind its head. Then draw the shape of the wings and the huge, deadly claws. Draw the ridge above the dragon's eyes to give it a scary expression!

Step 4

Add the markings on the head, then shade the eyes and draw the teeth. Draw the lines on the dragon's chest, belly, and tail. Add detail to the claws and wings.

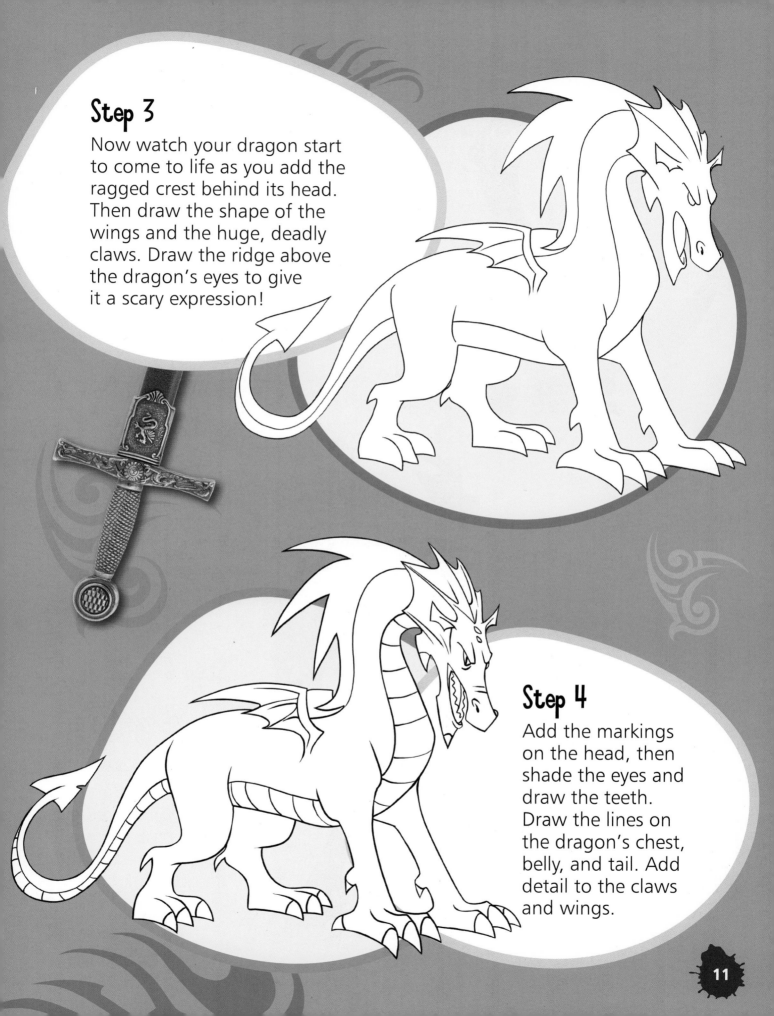

Step 5

Add shading to your dragon, remembering to include the claws, wings, and tail.

Step 6

Color your dragon's chest, belly, and the underside of its tail light blue. Use white for the claws and teeth. Give it red eyes and a pink tongue. Color the rest of the dragon dark blue.

Step 7

Add some touches of pink to the wings and the head crest. Then add highlights. Your terrifying dragon is complete.

Prize for a Dragon

In some old stories, villagers gave a young woman to an evil dragon so that it would leave their village alone. The unlucky girl was tied to a rock or a tree and left there for the wicked dragon to find!

Flying Dragons

With their enormous, powerful wings, dragons can leap into the sky at a moment's notice and soar high among the clouds. In many modern stories, people who have become friends with a dragon are even allowed to ride upon its back as the creature flies through the air!

Step 1

Draw your dragon in a flying pose. Draw the body, neck, and head. Draw the forelegs and hind legs. Then draw the wings and tail.

Step 2

Give your dragon a more finished outline, and draw its jaws wide open and scales on its back. Add the rough shape of the claws and the ears. Mark the eye. Erase any unwanted lines from step 1.

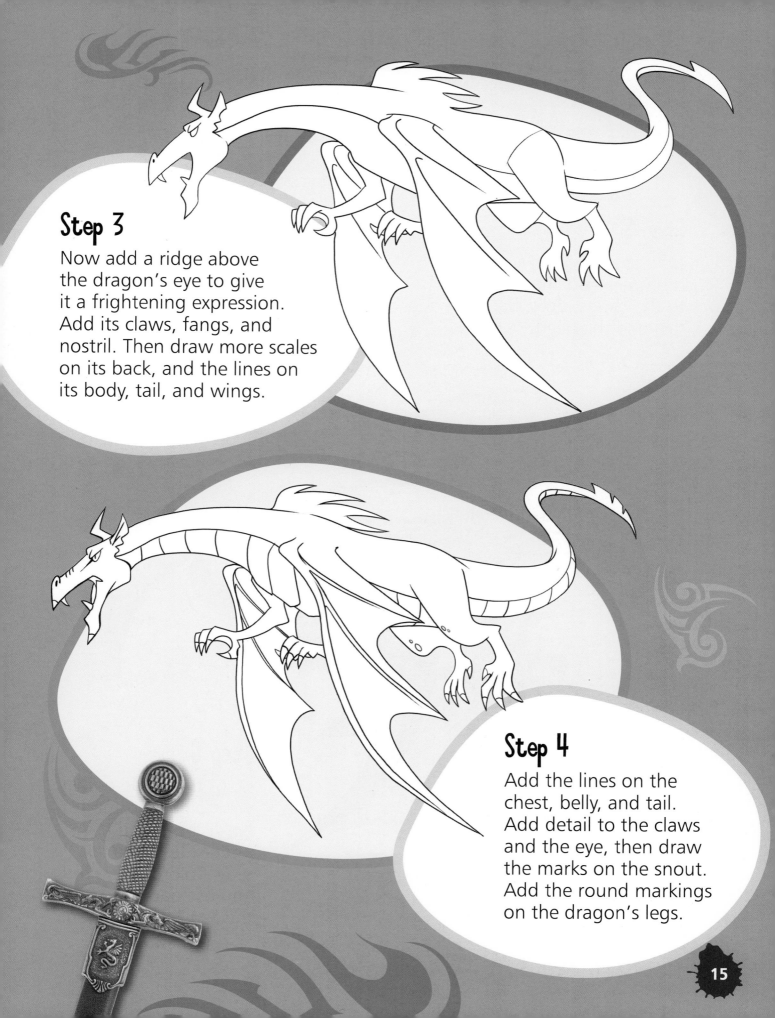

Step 3

Now add a ridge above the dragon's eye to give it a frightening expression. Add its claws, fangs, and nostril. Then draw more scales on its back, and the lines on its body, tail, and wings.

Step 4

Add the lines on the chest, belly, and tail. Add detail to the claws and the eye, then draw the marks on the snout. Add the round markings on the dragon's legs.

Step 5

Now shade your flying monster! Add shading to the wings, belly, back, tail, and the head.

Step 6

Color the inside right wing pink, and the belly, chest, and the underside of the tail gray. Color the eye red and use dark gray for the rest of the dragon.

Dragons and Wizards

Flying dragons are found in many old tales, but also in lots of modern stories, too. In *Harry Potter*, the young wizard must take on an enormous, sky-sweeping dragon!

Step 7

Add some touches of pink to the outside of the left wing. Then add some highlights to the back, ears, head, tail, body, and legs of your dragon. Add some highlights to the wings, too. Your monster is complete.

Fire-Breathing Dragons

Dragons are famous for breathing giant, hot flames. The mighty dragon can shoot a huge jet of flames from its mouth and nostrils. Angry dragons use their fire-breathing powers to turn anything in their path to cinders.

Step 1

Draw the dragon's body, then draw its legs, feet, neck, head, and tail. Add the wings and the flames shooting from the dragon's mouth.

Step 2

Go over your lines from step 1 to give the dragon a softer outline. Add its ears, eye, the shape of its feet, and its jaws. Draw the shape of the flames.

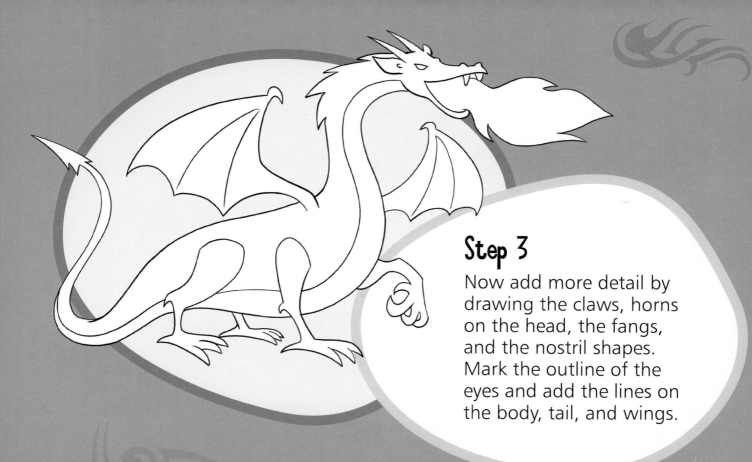

Step 3

Now add more detail by drawing the claws, horns on the head, the fangs, and the nostril shapes. Mark the outline of the eyes and add the lines on the body, tail, and wings.

Step 4

Draw the lines on the chest, belly, and tail. Then add the teeth and the lines around the right eye. Add detail to the ear, wings, claws, and flame.

Step 5

Shade your dragon's body, tail, head, and wings to start to bring it to life. Add shading to the flames, too.

Step 6

Color the belly, chest, and underside of the tail gold. Use gold and light yellow for the flames and the eye. Color the inside of the wings purple and the horns and claws gray. Color the rest of your dragon bright red.

Step 7

Add purple spots to your dragon's body and legs. Then add highlights to the fire-breathing beast to complete your scary picture.

Huge Serpents

The English word "dragon" comes from the French word, *dragon*. The word first came from an old Latin word, *draconem*, which means "huge serpent."

Water Dragons

Not all dragons live on land or fly high in the sky. Some dragons swim in water and live in lakes and oceans. These terrifying beasts lie hidden beneath the water's surface, only to rise up from their watery homes to feast on passersby!

Step 1

Draw this water dragon in a diving pose. Draw the body, neck, head, and tail. Then draw the wings and the tip of the fanned tail.

Step 2

Now go over the rough lines from step 1 to give your dragon a rounded outline. Then erase any unwanted lines. Draw the scales on the dragon's head, neck, and back, and roughly mark the eye.

Step 3

Draw the mouth and the scales on the jaw. Add detail to the eye and the lines on the body, wings, and tail.

Step 4

Now draw the lines on the neck, belly, and tail. Draw the gills at the side of the monster's head and the detailed lines on its wings and scales.

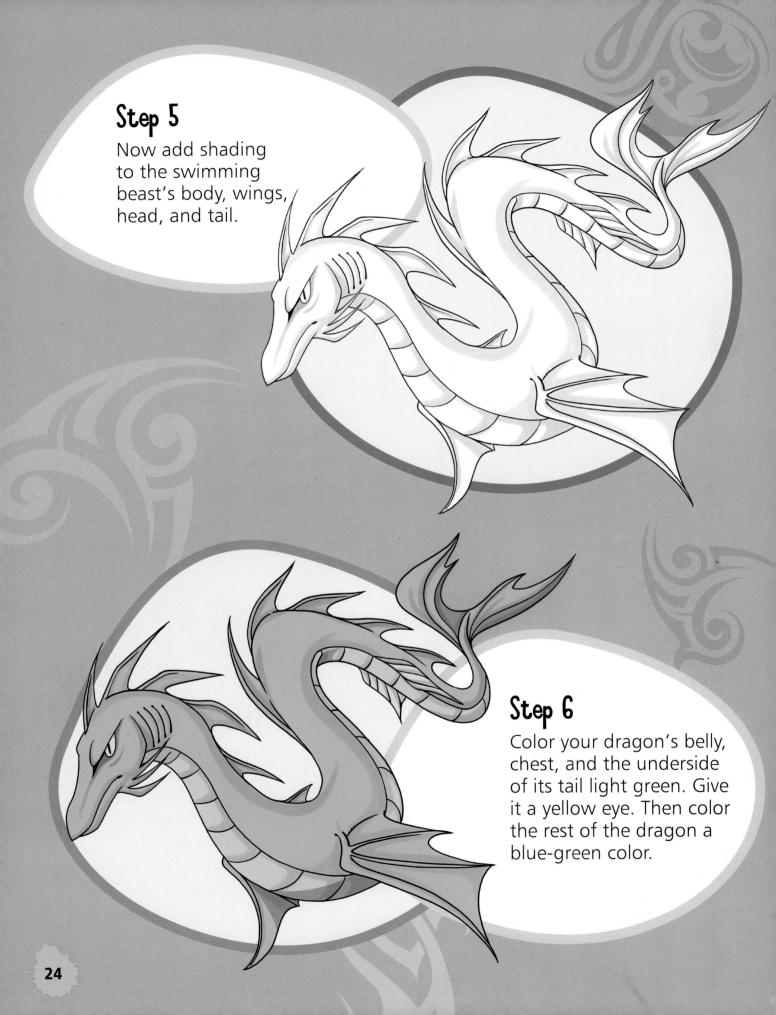

Step 5

Now add shading to the swimming beast's body, wings, head, and tail.

Step 6

Color your dragon's belly, chest, and the underside of its tail light green. Give it a yellow eye. Then color the rest of the dragon a blue-green color.

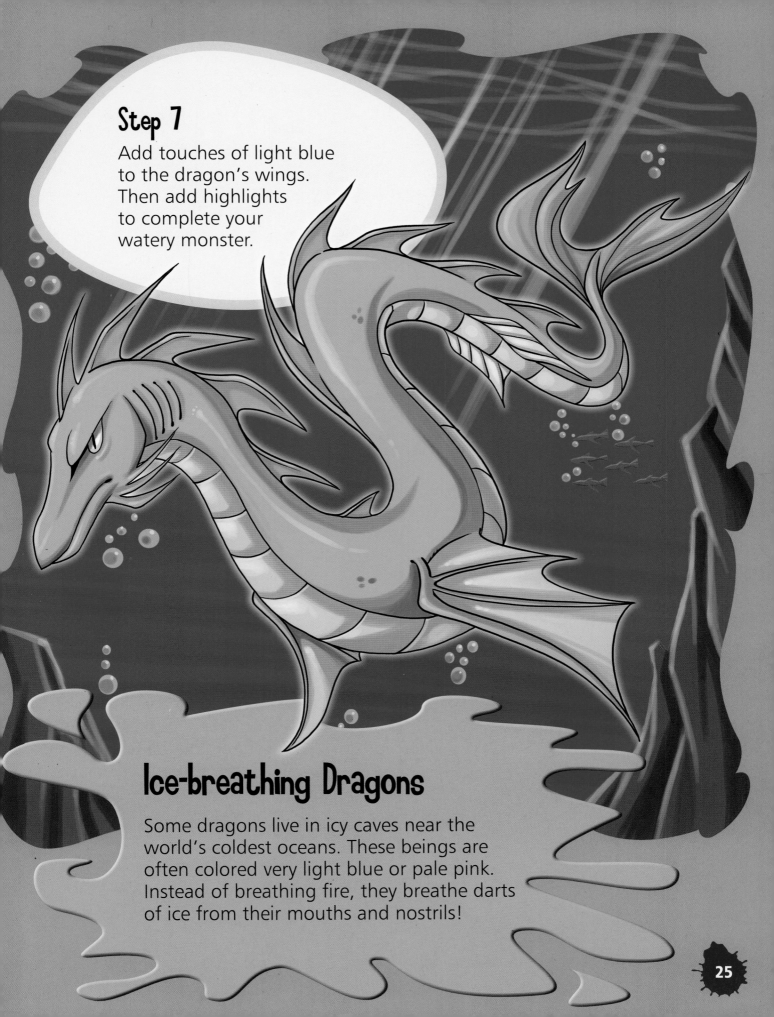

Step 7

Add touches of light blue to the dragon's wings. Then add highlights to complete your watery monster.

Ice-breathing Dragons

Some dragons live in icy caves near the world's coldest oceans. These beings are often colored very light blue or pale pink. Instead of breathing fire, they breathe darts of ice from their mouths and nostrils!

Chinese Dragons

In Chinese stories, all dragons live near water. The Chinese dragon does not have wings. These dragons are great friends of people and are said to protect them. The Chinese believe that dragons bring people good luck.

Step 1

Draw the dragon's body, neck, head, and tail. Then draw its legs. Draw its feet, using a crescent for the raised foot.

Step 2

Go over the rough lines from step 1 to give your dragon a more rounded outline. Mark the claws, shape the tail tip, and add the horns, eye, jaws, and nostril. Erase any unwanted lines.

Step 3

Now add detail to your picture. Give the dragon scales along its neck and tail, then add scales to its legs. Add detail to the claws and horns, and draw the outline of the eye. Then add the whiskers.

Step 4

Complete the claws and add the lines on the neck, chest, and belly. Add the ridges on the nose, the nostrils, and the jagged teeth. Then add scales to the chin and the jaws.

Step 5

Shade your awesome Chinese dragon. Add shading to the body, then use shading to bring out the detail of the dragon's amazing head and jaws.

Step 6

Color the jaw scales, chest, belly, and underside of the tail cream. Then use a red-brown for the whiskers and the rest of the scales. Color the eyes yellow and use light brown for the horns. Use green for the rest of the dragon.

Step 7

Add some dark green spots to the dragon's body, then add highlights to complete your lucky dragon.

Cloud Breather

Chinese dragons do not breathe fire or ice. Instead, these creatures breathe soft, billowing clouds from their mouths and nostrils! The Chinese believe that dragons are ruled by one wise and all-powerful dragon king.

29

Glossary

ancient very old

billowing throwing out lots of something, such as smoke or fire

cinders the ashes left behind when something has been burned

claws hard, sharp points on a creature's feet

crescent a long, curved shape that looks a little like a half moon

darts very thin, sharp objects that are fired as weapons

deadly able to kill

detail the fine lines on a drawing

disguise to try to look like something or someone else

erase to remove

evil bad

forelegs the legs at the front of a creature's body

highlights the light parts on a picture

horns sharp points on a creature's head

jaws the area of a creature's head in which the teeth are found

jet a powerful stream of air, gas, water, or flames

lairs the homes of animals

Latin a very old language that comes from Italy

magical to do with magic

mighty strong and powerful

modern not long ago

nostrils the openings on an animal's head through which it breathes

passersby people nearby or people who are walking past

pose the position a person or creature is in

protect to keep safe from harm

ridge a hard, bony area that is raised on a creature's body

scorching burning

serpent a snakelike creature with scaly skin and a tail

shading the dark markings on a picture

soar to fly easily high in the sky

tales stories

terrifying very scary

wicked bad

wise very smart

wizards men who can perform magic

For More Information

Books

Dobrzycki, Michael. *Drawing Dragons: A Complete Drawing Kit for Beginners*. Minneapolis, MN: Walter Foster, 2012.

Levin, Freddy. *1-2-3 Draw Knights, Castles, and Dragons*. Mankato, MN: Peel Press, 2001.

Staple, Sandra. *Drawing Dragons: Learn How to Create Fantastic Fire-Breathing Dragons*. Berkley, CA: Ulysses Press, 2008.

Websites

Find out how to train a dragon at:
www.howtotrainyourdragonbooks.com

Discover lots of fun dragon art activities at:
www.activityvillage.co.uk/dragons_theme.htm

Find even more dragons to draw at:
www.hellokids.com/r_1959/draw/drawing-tutorials-step-by-step/dragons-for-kids

Publisher's note to educators and parents: Our editors have carefully reviewed these websites to ensure that they are suitable for students. Many websites change frequently, however, and we cannot guarantee that a site's future contents will continue to meet our high standards of quality and educational value. Be advised that students should be closely supervised whenever they access the Internet.

Index